Daniel Fast Metabolism Smoothies: 39 FAST and EASY Smoothies (All Under 200), Lose 7 Pounds in 7 Days and Boost Your Metabolism.

by John McDonalds

Disclaimer

The information provided in this book is designed to provide helpful information on the subjects discussed. The publisher and author are not responsible for any specific health or allergy needs that may require medical supervision and are not liable for any damages or negative consequences from any treatment, action, application or preparation, to any person reading or following the information in this book.

References are provided for informational purposes only and do not constitute endorsement of any websites or other sources. Readers should be aware that the websites listed in this book may change.

Table of Contents

Introduction

Thanks for purchasing 'Daniel Fast Shred Smoothies'

This collection of recipes is perfect for those on the Daniel Fast. Whether you're looking for a quick nutritious breakfast or a powerful "meal replacement", you'll find the recipe you're looking for.

As with any smoothie, many additives can be added for a variety of reasons. You can add any powdered product and it won't affect taste, such as protein powder, wheat germ, oatmeal, 100% bran cereal, soy powder, rice powder, flaxseed oil, bee pollen, etc. All of these products are available in health food stores.

You can throw just about anything in a smoothie to enhance its flavor such as honey, tofu, jams, any combination of fruits, peanut butter, juices, etc., but keep in mind it will affect the nutritional values listed below. However, you wouldn't have to worry about any addictive, because these Smoothies I've prepared for you are natural and Very delicious. They're easy to make, good for you, and really delicious. The fun part is that you can make tons of different variations.

Well ok then! I made a lot of Smoothies while fasting. I put a lot of time and effort into this cookbook and hope you enjoy them as much as I do. For most of the recipes, all you need is a blender. Plus, you'll save lots of money by making these healthy smoothies instead of buying expensive protein bars, which usually have lots of additives and usually taste like chalk.

You'll never go back to protein bars, once you start making these nutritious smoothies.

Enjoy and happy 'smoothing'.

Daniel Fast Overview

Daniel fast is based on partial fast as mentioned in the Scripture. If one needs to enter the spiritual disciple of prayer and fasting, you should go on Daniel fast. There are two scriptures that advice two types of Daniel fasts.

In those days I, Daniel, was mourning three full weeks. I ate no pleasant food, no meat or wine came into my mouth, nor did I anoint myself at all, till three whole weeks were fulfilled." (Daniel 10:1-2)

Please test your servants for ten days, and let them give us vegetables to eat and water to drink." (Daniel 1:12)

The first fast is based on 2 Kings 24 which lasts for 10 days and you can eat only vegetables, fruits and drink only water and the other is based on Daniel fast, which last for 21 days, where you need to abstain from Kings meal. The Kings meals consists of breads, meat, and wine. So you would need to abstain from all meat and wine for the Daniel Fast.

This fast was inspired by Daniel and his companion, when they were taken into captive and given vegetable and water. They looked mentally and physically healthy, compared to those provided with the king's meal and wine daily.

Thus, this diet came to be known as Daniel fast (Daniel plan). Today, Daniel Fast is followed for two major reason. One of the reason is to detox the body, shred fat, boost your metabolism, lose weight and feel great. While the other is to maintain a closer relationship and enhance your spiritual life with God.

You need to consult your doctor about it first, if you too are looking to trying the Daniel fast. If you get a go ahead from your Doctor, then you can begin with the fast. Daniel fast supports healthy eating and therefore will be supported by your doctor.

Daniel Fast Smoothies

Breakfast smoothies are perfect for the Daniel Diet. Everyone loves a great smoothie! I made lots of smoothies while I was on the fast and it really helped me stay on the fast, while I lose weight and drew closer to God. Smoothies are quick to make, provides lots of nutrients and delicious! Check out this recipe I've put together of how to prepare a healthy, low calories smoothie – The Daniel Fast style!

Berry Shred Smoothie

Get the energy you need to start up the Day with this easy-to-make drink.

SERVINGS: 1

Calories Per Servings: 162.5

Ingredients:

1 cup blueberries

1½ cup chopped strawberries

1 tsp fresh lemon juice

½ cup raspberries

½ cup ice cubes

2 Tbsp. honey

How You make it:

Place all the Ingredients in a blender and blend until Smooth. Serve Chilled.

Shred Sunset Smoothie

Blend peach and apricot together, and your smoothie will looks like an early-morning sunrise.

SERVINGS: 4

Calories Per Servings: 130

Ingredients:

½ c club soda, chilled

1 cup apricot nectar, chilled

1 banana

1 container (8 oz.) low-fat peach yogurt(Soy or Almond Milk)

1 Tbsp. frozen lemonade concentrate

How you Make it:

1. COMBINE the apricot nectar, banana, yogurt (Soy or Almond Milk), and lemonade concentrate. Process for 30 seconds, or until creamy and smooth.

2. STIR in the club soda and serve immediately.

Daniel Fast Green Smoothies

Take this Delicious low calorie green smoothie and watch the fat melt off!

Servings: 2

Calories Per Servings: 160

Ingredients:

4 cucumber slices, peeled

6 ice cubes

2 handfuls of fresh spinach, arugula or romaine

1 fresh or frozen banana

1 apple, quartered

1 Tsp. cinnamon

1 Tsp. honey

Water as desired

1 cup coconut water (Almond or Soy milk)

How You Make it:

Mix all the ingredients in a blender and blend until Smooth. Serve Immediately.

Berry Vanilla Special

Fat-free vanilla yogurt sweetens this tangy fruit smoothie.

SERVINGS: 2

Calories Per Servings: 192

Ingredients:

1 c (8 oz.) fat-free vanilla yogurt

½ c frozen unsweetened raspberries

¾ c unsweetened pineapple juice

½ c frozen unsweetened strawberries

How You Make It:

COMBINE all the Ingredients, strawberries, raspberries, and pineapple juice.
Add the yogurt. Blend until smooth.

Fruity-Juicy Smoothie

A splash of orange juice infuses summer citrus into this healthy and refreshing snack.

SERVINGS: 2

Calories Per Servings: 140

Ingredients:

½ c canned crushed pineapple in juice

½ c loose-pack mixed frozen berries or strawberries

½ c sliced ripe banana

½ c plain yogurt

½ c orange juice

How You Make It:

Mix the pineapple (with juice), berries, yogurt, banana, and orange juice in a food processor fitted with the metal blade, in a blender, or in a large measuring cup with an immersion blender. Blend or Process for about 2 minutes, or until smooth.

Vanilla Ginger Smoothie

Soothe nausea, heartburn, digestion, and other stomach trouble with the fresh ginger in this natural remedy drink.

SERVINGS: 2

Calories Per Servings: 157

Ingredients:

1 banana, sliced

¾ c (6 Oz) vanilla yogurt

½ tsp freshly grated ginger

1 Tbsp honey

How You Make It:

COMBINE the yogurt, banana, honey, and ginger. Blend until smooth.

Orange Flavored Creamsicle

Need to cool down after a tough workout or a hot day at the beach? Lap up this low-cal, citrus-infused drink. While enjoying the "Dream Flavor".

SERVINGS: 1

Calories Per Servings: 160

Ingredients:

1 navel orange, peeled

2 Tbsp. frozen orange juice concentrate

4 ice cubes

¼ c fat-free half-and-half or fat-free yogurt

¼ tsp vanilla extract

How You Make It:

Mix all the ingredients, the orange, half-and-half or yogurt, orange juice concentrate, vanilla, and ice cubes in a Blender. Process until smooth.

Merry-Berry Breakfast

Merry-Berry Breakfast Smoothies. Start your day off with a bang with this fruit-packed smoothie.

SERVINGS: 2

Calories Per Servings: 112

Ingredients:

2 tsp finely grated fresh ginger

1 c frozen unsweetened raspberries

¼ c frozen pitted unsweetened cherries or raspberries

¾ c chilled unsweetened almond or rice milk

1½ Tbsp. honey

2 tsp fresh lemon juice

1 tsp ground flaxseed.

How You Make It:

Mix all ingredients in blender. After mixing, add lemon juice to taste. Puree until smooth. Pour into 2 chilled glasses, and Serve.

Straw-Kiwi-Berry Smoothie

Stay full and fight disease. While on the Daniel Fast. This high-fiber drink with low calories becomes even healthier when you use organic kiwis, which contain higher levels of heart-healthy vitamin C and polyphenols.

SERVINGS: 4

Calories Per Servings: 87

Ingredients:

1 kiwifruit, sliced

1¼ c cold apple juice

1 ripe banana, sliced

1½ tsp honey

5 frozen strawberries

How You Make It:

COMBINE the kiwifruit, juice, strawberries, banana, and honey. Puree until smooth. Serve Immediately.

.

Blueberry-Soy Special Smoothie

Succulent, summer-ripe blueberries burst with flavor in this delicious drink. Skip the sugar or artificial sweetener for a healthier pick; the fruit makes it naturally sweet.

SERVINGS: 2

Calories Per Servings: 125

Ingredients:

1 tsp pure vanilla extract

½ frozen banana, sliced

½ c frozen loose-pack blueberries

2 tsp sugar or 2 packets artificial sweetener

1¼ c light soy milk

How You Make It:

Mix 1 cup of the soy milk, the banana, blueberries, vanilla extract, and sugar or sweetener. Blend until smooth for about 20 to 30 seconds. Add up to one-quarter (1/4) cup more milk if a thinner smoothie is desired. Serve Immediately.

Peach Perfect Smoothies

Fat-free vanilla ice cream makes this dish slimming and sinful. You can Skip the spoonful of sugar for a healthier pick.

SERVINGS: 2

Calories Per Serving: 150

Ingredients:

½ c strawberries

2 tsp whey protein powder

1 c 1% milk

2 Tbsp. low-fat vanilla yogurt

½ c frozen peaches

3 ice cubes

⅛ tsp powdered ginger

How to Make It:

1. **BLEND** together the milk, juice, yogurt, all liquid ingredients and protein powder; this will make sure it's evenly distributed and help break down the grainy powder.

2. **ADD** mushy ingredients, like precooked oatmeal and fruit, then add ice at the end.

3. However, you can toss in more ice cubes, for a thicker shake; you'll add volume without the calories.

Watermelon Smoothie

This is a very yummy smoothie. Transform a summer fruit favorite into a drinkable delight. Just remember to buy seedless watermelon or remove the seeds before you blend!

SERVINGS: 2

Calories Per Servings: 56

Ingredients:

¼ cup fat-free milk

2 cup ice

2 cup chopped watermelon

How You Make it:

1. **Mix** the milk and watermelon, and blend until smooth, or for 15 seconds.

2. Add the ice, and puree or blend 20 seconds longer, or to your desired consistency.

3. Add more ice, if needed, and blend for 10 seconds.

Sunrise Special Smoothie

This smoothie look like an early morning rise, when banana and apricot are blended together.

SERVINGS: 4

Calories Per Servings: 135

Ingredients:

1 Tbsp. frozen lemonade concentrate

1 cup apricot nectar, chilled

1 banana

½ cup club soda, chilled

1 container (8 oz) low-fat peach yogurt

How You Make It:

1. **Mix** all the ingredients, and lemonade concentrate.

2. Process for 30 seconds, or until smooth and creamy.

3. Serve immediately, after **Stirring** in the club soda.

Ultimate Shape Smoothie

Wonderfully thick and tasty, good for those who wants to slim-down and get in shape. This drink easily substitutes for milkshakes and ice cream.

SERVINGS: 1

Calories Per Servings: 185

Ingredients:

1 cup frozen berries, such as blueberries, raspberries, or strawberries

½ cup orange juice or other juice

½ cup low-fat yogurt (any flavor)

How You Make it:

1. **Mix** the yogurt, berries, and orange juice in a blender and pulse for 30 seconds.

2. Blend until smooth, or for 30 seconds.

Cherry-Berry Smoothie

Thanks to low-glycemic strawberries and cherries, this frothy "milkshake" seems indulgent but makes a smart snack. Antioxidants in the fruit and calcium in the yogurt add nutritional punch.

SERVINGS: 2

Calories Per Serving: 98

Ingredients:

½ cup frozen sweet cherries (we used Earthbound Farm Organic)

½ cup chilled unsweetened vanilla almond milk

½ cup 2% plain Greek-style yogurt

¼-½ cup ice cubes

1 cup frozen strawberries

How You Make It:

Mix all the ingredients and puree until smooth in high-power blender. Divide between 2 glasses. Serve Immediately.

Coco-Mango Power-Up

Rehydrate after exercise with potassium and other electrolytes from mango and coconut water. This is a very Delicious Smoothie for the Daniel Fast. Yogurt and almonds provide muscle-repairing protein.

SERVINGS: 2.5

Calories Per Serving: 181

Ingredients:

¼ cup frozen strawberries (about 5)

¾ cup coconut water

½ cup 2% plain Greek-style yogurt

1¼ cup frozen mango chunks

1 Tbsp. fresh lemon juice

2 Tbsp. almond meal (ground almonds)

How You Make It:

Combine all the ingredients and puree until smooth, in high-power blender.

Divide between 2 glasses. Serve Immediately

Cocoa-Berry Chiller

The unsweetened cacao nibs or cocoa powder, serves as a good sources of antioxidants.

SERVINGS: 2

Calories Per Servings: 105

Ingredients:

½ cup 2% plain Greek-style yogurt

½ cup chilled unsweetened vanilla almond milk

1 cup frozen strawberries

¼-½ cup ice cubes

½ cup unsweetened cacao nibs or cocoa powder.

How You Make It:

1.   Combine all the ingredients, yogurt, Strawberries, almond milk.

2.   In high-power blender and puree until smooth.

3.   Add unsweetened cacao nibs or cocoa powder.

4.   Divide between 2 glasses. Serve Immediately.

Peach-berry Specials

This smoothies is Very Yummy and Good for the Daniel Fast. You can always Substitute the peach fruits with frozen tropical fruit blend. Enjoy!

SERVINGS: 2

Calories Per Serving: 185

Ingredients:

½ cup 2% plain Greek-style yogurt

1¼ cup frozen Peaches

¾ cup coconut water

1 Tbsp. fresh lemon juice

¼ cup frozen strawberries (about 5)

2 Tbsp. almond meal (ground almonds)

How You Make It:

1. Mix all ingredients, yogurt, peaches, strawberries, almonds in high-power blender and puree until smooth.

Divide between 2 glasses. Serve.

Pump up the protein by adding raw almond butter or unsweetened whey protein powder plus a dash of pure vanilla extract.

Mango with Avocado Gem

The Mango in this Combo helps to boost Metabolism and help Shred Fat.

Servings: 2

Calories Per Serving: 191

Ingredients:

1/4 cup sliced avocado

1 cup sliced Champagne mango

1 tablespoon lime juice

1 tablespoon fresh mint

1 teaspoon honey

2 cups crushed ice

How To Make it:

Mix all the ingredients, lime juice, avocado, Champagne Mango, and Puree until Smooth.

Ginger with Berries Smoothie

Servings: 2

Calories Per Serving: 179

Ingredients:

1/4 cup prepared oatmeal

1/4 cup 1% low-fat milk

1/2 teaspoon grated fresh ginger

1 cup fresh blackberries

1/2 cup sliced strawberries

1 teaspoon honey

1/2 cup ice

How To Make It:

Mix all the Ingredients in a high-power blender, and blend till Smooth. Divide in two cups and Serve.

Santé Smoothies

Servings: 2

Calories Per Servings: 184

Ingredients:

2/3 cup frozen sliced peaches

2/3 cup frozen mango pieces

2/3 cup peach nectar

1 tablespoon honey

1 (6-ounce) carton organic peach fat-free yogurt

How you Make it:

Place frozen mango pieces, frozen sliced peaches, cup peach nectar, 1 tablespoon honey, and 1 (6-ounce) carton organic peach fat-free yogurt in a blender; until smooth, for about 2 minutes. Serve immediately.

Amazing APPLE PIE SMOOTHIE

Servings: 2

Calories Per Serving: 198

Ingredients:

1/2 teaspoons cinnamon

1 frozen banana

1/2 peeled, chopped apple

1 cup apple juice

Pinch of nutmeg

How You Make It:

1. Blend all ingredients in a Blender, until smooth.

2. Great substitute for applesauce! Control the consistency by adding more or less chopped apple.

Green Smoothies

Servings: 2

Calories Per Serving: 162

Ingredients:

1 cup fresh baby spinach leaves

1 1/2 cups chopped fresh honeydew

1/3 cup non-fat vanilla Greek yogurt

How You Make It:

Mix all Ingredients in a blender, Puree until Smooth. Enjoy the wonderful Taste.

BANANA ORANGE CREAM SMOOTHIE

SERVINGS: 1

Calories Per Serving: 175

Ingredients:

1/4 cup orange juice

1 tbsp. coconut milk

1/4 cup pineapple juice

1/2 banana

1/2 cup crushed ice or 2 small ice cubes

1/4 tsp grated fresh ginger root

How You Make It:

Add all ingredients, orange juice, coconut milk, Pineapple juice, banana, to blender and process until smooth. Serve Immediately.

Banana Fruity Smoothie

Servings: 2

Calories Per Servings: 188

Ingredients:

1 ripe peach, halved, pitted, peeled, and diced

1 1/2 cups freshly squeezed orange juice

1 half banana, peeled and cut into 1-inch pieces

3 ice cubes

1 cup raspberries.

How You Make It:

Mix all the ingredients, banana, peach, raspberries, orange juice, in blender and whip until smooth. Serve Chilled.

Peach Refresher

Servings: 2

Calories Per Serving: 180

Ingredients:

1 cup Chilled peach nectar

½ cup Soy Milk

Ground nutmeg

1 Container (6 ounces) peach yogurt.

How You Make It:

1. Combine all ingredients nectar, Soy milk and yogurt in blender.
2. Cover and blend on high speed until smooth for about 30 seconds.
3. Sprinkle with nutmeg. 2 servings (about 1-1/4 cups each); 180 calories per serving.

Pina Colada Slush Smoothie

SERVINGS: 2

Calories Per Serving: 190

Ingredients:

2 cups cubed fresh pineapple

1-1/2 cups pineapple juice, chilled

1 cup vanilla fat-free frozen yogurt

1/4 cup cream of coconut

1 cup ice cubes

How You Make It:

1. Place pineapple into freezer; freeze until firm for about an hour.
2. Take out of the freezer; Allow to stand for 10 minutes.
3. Combine cream and juice in a blender.
4. With blender on, add the ice cubes and pineapple, one at a time; process until smooth.
5. Add yogurt; process until smooth.
6. Serve immediately.

Cantaloupe Pineapple Smoothie

SERVINGS: 2

Calories Per Serving: 177

Ingredients:

1 1/2 cups diced cantaloupe

1 1/2 cups diced pineapple

1/2 cup freshly squeezed orange juice

1/2 cup carrot juice

3 ice cubes

Pinch nutmeg

How You Make It:

Combine all ingredients, pineapple, cantaloupe, carrot juice, orange juice in blender and whip until smooth. Serve Immediately.

Fruity Delight Smoothie

SERVINGS: 1

Calories Per Serving: 197

Ingredients:

1/2 cup hulled strawberries (Use without cutting up)

1 frozen banana (best if cut into 1-inch-chunks then frozen)

Cinnamon to taste

1/4 cup soy milk, orange juice or water

How You Make It:

1. Combine all of the ingredients in a blender.

2. You can start with one-quarter cup of liquid and add more depending on how thick you want the smoothie. 3. Blend in spurts until smooth.

Note: You can vary the flavor by also Using peaches, apple slices, blueberries, or more bananas in place of strawberries (or combine them!) Use fresh bananas and 1-2 ice cubes. You May need to vary the liquid depending on the juiciness of the fruit. In addition to the cinnamon, add one or more of: ginger, nutmeg, cloves, vanilla vegan.

Raspberry Cappuccino Smoothie

SERVINGS: 2

Calories Per Serving: 169

Ingredients:

2 tablespoon chocolate syrup

1/3 cup fresh-brewed espresso

1 1/2 cup nonfat coffee flavor frozen yogurt

1/4 teaspoon cocoa powder

1 cup raspberries

3/4 cup chocolate milk, low-fat

1/2 cup soy milk

How You Make It:

1. Combine the espresso, chocolate milk, and chocolate syrup in a blender.
2. Add the raspberries and frozen yogurt.
3. Blend until smooth.
4. Pour into glasses.

5. Rinse out the blender container.

6. Pour the Soy milk into the blender and blend on high speed about 15 seconds, until frothy.

7. Divide between the smoothies and sprinkle them with chocolate powder. Serve Chilled.

Pineapple Special

Servings: 2

Calories Per Serving: 128

Ingredients:

8-10 frozen boysenberries

1/4 cup pineapple juice

6 fresh strawberries

2 pineapple rings (Dole pineapple slices)

3 oz. non-fat yogurt, any flavor (about half a container of Yoplait)

12-15 frozen raspberries

1 cup orange juice

12-15 frozen blueberries

Add Ice as desired.

How You Make It:

Add all ingredients into blender. Blend well until desired smoothie consistency is reached!

Serve Chilled.

Rich Berry Smoothie

Antioxidant-rich green tea makes this smoothie a nutritional powerhouse. This Smoothie is always cherished by Friends and Family and very healthy.

SERVINGS: 2

Calories Per Serving: 135

Ingredients:

¾ cup calcium fortified light vanilla soy milk

2 tsp honey

3 Tbsp. water

1 green tea bag

1½ cup frozen blueberries

½ med banana

How You Make It:

1. Heat the water on high in a small bowl until steaming hot. Add tea bag and allow to brew 3 minutes. Remove tea bag. Stir honey into tea until it dissolves.

2. Mix banana, berries, and milk in a blender with ice crushing ability.

3. ADD tea to blender. Blend ingredients at the highest setting until smooth, on ice crush. (Some blenders may require additional water to process the mixture.) Pour smoothie into tall glass and serve Chilled.

Everyone's Delight Smoothie

Slurp down this smoothie at breakfast, and you'll feel satisfied until lunchtime. This is the World's Best Smoothie!

SERVINGS: 2

Calories Per Serving: 150

Ingredients:

1 banana

6 frozen strawberries

1 cup plain nonfat yogurt

½ cup orange juice

How You Make It:

Mix the banana, yogurt, juice, and strawberries and puree for about 20 seconds. Scrape down the sides and blend for an additional 15 seconds. Serve Chilled.

Pineapple Purity

This decadently thick drink can even satisfy your desire for ice cream! Everyone loves a healthy a creamy Smoothie, Try this and feel the Passion of pineapple.

SERVINGS: 2

Calories Per Serving: 142

Ingredients:

1 cup pineapple chunks

1 cup low-fat or light vanilla yogurt

6 ice cubes

How You Make It:

1. **Mix** the ice cubes and yogurt. Blend, pulsing as needed, until the ice is in large chunks.

2. **ADD** the pineapple to the mixture and blend at high speed until smooth.

3. **Serve** Chilled.

South Beach Perfection

Thick like a milkshake, this coconut-infused smoothie transports you to a tropical island. The South Beach Perfect Sip.

SERVINGS: 2

Calories Per Serving: 149.5

Ingredients:

½ cup fresh pineapple chunks

1 papaya, cut into chunks

½ cup crushed ice

1 tsp ground flaxseed

1 tsp coconut extract

1 cup fat-free plain yogurt

How You Make It:

COMBINE all the ingredients in a blender, pineapple, papaya, yogurt, ice cube, flaxseed, and coconut extract. Process until smooth and frosty for about 30 seconds.

Mango-Apricot Appeal

Fresh lemon juice adds a tangy splash to this sweet smoothie. This is so Delicious, you would want to have an Extra Glass every Minute of the Day.

SERVINGS: 3

Calories Per Serving: 152

Ingredients:

1 cup reduced-fat milk or plain low-fat yogurt

2 ripe mangoes, 10 to 12 ounces each, peeled and chopped (about 2 c)

4 tsp fresh lemon juice

Lemon peel twists (garnish)

¼ tsp vanilla extract

6 apricots, peeled, pitted, and chopped (about 2 cup)

8 ice cubes.

How You Make It:

1. Combine the mangoes, apricots, milk or lemon juice, yogurt, and vanilla extract in a blender. Process for 8 seconds. Add the ice cubes, and process until smooth, for about 6 to 8 seconds longer.

2. POUR the mix into 3 glasses, if desired, garnish with lemon twists, and serve immediately.

Daniel's Luscious Smoothie

To eliminate processed sugar, this reader created a sweet, sugar-free smoothie. This is Good smoothie for those on the Fast, and can replace meals, anytime, anywhere.

SERVINGS: 2

Calories Per Serving: 123

Ingredients:

1 cup frozen, unsweetened strawberries

1 cup skim milk

1 Tbsp. sunflower or pumpkin seeds (optional)

1 Tbsp. cold-pressed organic flaxseed oil

How You Make It:

1. Combine frozen strawberries and milk in a blender for a minute.

2. Pour the mix into a glass serve with a tablespoon of sunflower or pumpkin seeds, or stir in the tablespoon of flaxseed oil instead.

Soy Special Smoothie

Skipping breakfast can leave you starving mid-morning, and makes you reach for tempting junk food. Instead, sip this on-the-go soy smoothie.

SERVINGS: 2

Calories Per Serving: 175

Ingredients:

1 frozen banana, sliced

½ cup frozen blueberries

1 cup calcium-fortified vanilla soy milk

½ cup corn flakes cereal.

How You Make It:

COMBINE the blueberries, milk, banana and cereals in a blender for 20 seconds. Scrape down the sides and blend for an additional 15 seconds. Serve Immediately.

Mango Delight Smoothie

Take advantage of ripe mangoes disease-fighting ability with this delicious drink. Everyone loves a healthy Delicious Smoothie.

SERVINGS: 2.5

Calories Per Serving: 125

Ingredients:

1 cup fat-free frozen vanilla yogurt

1 can (8 oz.) juice-packed pineapple chunks

1 gram ripe mango, peeled and chopped

Crushed or cracked ice

1 ripe banana, sliced

How You Make It:

1. COMBINE the frozen yogurt, pineapple (with juice), banana and mango. Blend until smooth.

2. Gradually drop in enough ice to bring the level up to 4 cups, with the blender running. Blend until the ice is pureed. Serve Immediately.

Conclusion

In my quest to lose weight, I have tried a lot of diet fad out there, some which sounded too good to be true, while some other I wasn't able to keep up with. However, the Daniel Fast helped me achieve big result, losing 7 pound in 7days. That was a miracle for me, you could achieve that too, if you follow religiously to the 21 Day Daniel Fast.

This Fasting has been followed by millions of people as a way of cleansing the spirit from past faults, wrong deeds and bad habits of giving in to temptations.

If you enjoyed this book, please take the time to share your thoughts and post a positive review with 5 star rating on Amazon, it would encourage me and make me serve you better. It'd be greatly appreciated!

Thank you and God Bless!

Books on Health & Fitness Diets
RECOMMENDED BOOK FROM THE SAME AUTHOR:

Are you looking for a Way to lose weight and keep it off for a long time while deepening your relationship with God? Then this is for you,

Get Daniel Fast Shred Diet Recipes: 35 Easy-To-Cook healthy recipes, lose 7 pounds in 7 days on the Daniel Plan. For Just $0.99 Today, for a limited Time.

Lose 7 pounds in 7 days, discover the insider secret... Click on the Link below to buy Now!

http://www.amazon.com/Daniel-Shred-Recipes-Easy---Cook-ebook/dp/B00IADVBIO/

Who else wants to Experience the Incredible taste of the World's Best Sauce...?

Welcome the Brand New, Never Heard Before -<u>The Ultimate Sriracha Hot Sauce- 25 Easy-to-Cook Healthy Recipes with This "Rooster Sauce"</u>

CLICK HERE TO BUY:

http://www.amazon.com/dp/B00HLJWWIQ

The Pound a Day Diet Recipes: 61 easy-to-cook healthy Recipes to Help with Your Diet On A Budget...Loose that pound today eating the foods you love

Recommended for the Pound a Day Dieters

CLICK HERE TO BUY ON AMAZON:

http://bookShow.me/B00HXYU736

As Seen on T.V- **Super Shred Diet Recipes: 61 Easy-to-cook Healthy Recipes To Help you Lose weight FAST in 4weeks.** This Book would give you lovely Recipe Ideas for Dr. Ian Smith Super Shred Program.

CLICK HERE TO BUY:

http://www.amazon.com/dp/B00HSLGOG8

CPSIA information can be obtained at www.ICGtesting.com
Printed in the USA
LVOW11s2051290714

396584LV00001B/321/P